Jump Start

Tune Up Your Life with Prayer and Affirmations

SYLVIA L. MORSON

JUMP START: Tune Up Your Life with Prayer And Affirmations

Published By: www.advisedbyamber.com

Printed in the United States of America

ISBN-13: 978-1-7376698-0-7

I dedicate this book to my God, Jesus Christ and Holy Spirit.

To my husband Pastor Doran, children Doran Jr., Dalisa and Amber, and grandchildren Bailee and Brooke.

To my family, friends and Higher Praise Worship Center (Detroit, MI).

CONTENTS

FOREWORD

With life as we know it, we need to result to prayer more than anything to revive ourselves. No self-help book, life coach, degree, or therapist alone will ever be enough to help you revive what has been dead or idle for so long in your life. Only God is powerful enough to restore life into dead relationships, self-hatred, low self-esteem, poverty, broken hearts, and so on. For some of us, we've spent decades ignoring all the signs urging us to seek a tune up. Why? It's because it is always easier to place the blame or focus on others than to accept the fact that our own toxic thinking and habits have created the life we are living in this present moment.

Luke 6:41 says *"And why worry about a speck in your friend's eye when you have a log in your own?"* For context, a speck is roughly 0.5 microns which is probably not much bigger than the period used at the end of this sentence. However, a log on average measures at 16 inches. Know that while you may be passionate about "helping others" you can't effectively do so until you allow God to help you shed inches off your log by renewing his spirit within you. For in Luke 6:45 it tells us that *"A good person produces good things from the treasury of a good heart, and an evil person produces evil things from the treasury of an evil heart. What you say flows from what is in your heart."* Now that you have set out to read **Jump Start** by author **Sylvia Morson**, you can no longer ignore the signs.

This book is a great opportunity to give not only your heart but your life a sincere tune up. This book uncovers all the depths of our feelings and thoughts which allow us to come to God in spirit and in truth. Sylvia Morson, who authors this book also had a hand in authoring my life as she just so happens to be my mother (spoiler alert). With that being said, I seen first-hand her life be a testament that our words do have power. In this book she takes you through not only time in prayer but helps you to build new habits by the words you speak through daily affirmations.

It is my prayer, that as you journey through this book, God will jump start areas in your life you didn't even realize needed reviving. I pray that your soul finds rest and your life restoration in Christ Jesus. I pray that you humble yourself enough to be real with God over these next 31 days. That you come to a place of repentance and self-reflection that allows you to cast years of insecurities, toxic behaviors and hidden motives on God. I find it fitting to encourage you to stop carrying what God never intended for you to – anger, bitterness, stress, and the weight of sin, that you either committed or was committed against you. Now is the time to get free.

Amber R. Morson
Author of No Prayer, No Power

INTRODUCTION

In the bible two passages of scriptures I often reflect upon on are Proverbs 18:21 which says "death and life *are* in the power of the tongue and they that love it shall eat the fruit thereof." Galatians 6:7 which says, "Be not deceived; God is not mocked: for whatsoever a man soweth, that shall he also reap."

I am a firm believer that the words you choose to release out of your mouth are like seeds planted into the ground that will produce a harvest. Whatever you have sown that is what your yielding crop will be. Your words can build or destroy character, can heal or cause pain, cause joy or sadness and make success or failure a way of life. The choice is yours, therefore, use caution before you speak.

At an early age my mother would sit me down and teach me the importance of guarding my mouth, how not to use profanity, to always think before I speak and to never speak words I really don't attend to say. She taught me that the power of words can influence my life and others around me. This was one rule in my household that I dare not break.

My parent's positive affirmations, spiritual guidance and leading by example helped to mold, shape and build a strong character and sense of myself-worth. As a young child my mentality and belief that I can do all things through Christ that strengthens me was not up for debate. Nothing could make me believe anything different.

As I grew into my young adult years my understanding became very clear of the scripture Luke 6:45 which says, " A good man out of the good treasure of his heart bringeth forth that which is good; and an evil man out of the evil treasure of his heart bringeth forth that which is evil for of the abundance of the heart his mouth speaketh." This reminded me that the heart and mouth are in connection with each other. I had to guard my heart against any damaged or unforgiveness emotions to ensure nothing negative or harmful came out of my mouth or in my actions. I was intentional about letting goodness spring forth out of it. I began to implement this knowledge into my way of living. I understood the importance of doing self-evaluations and the power of using my words to decree and declare the promises of God words over my life. I had to exercise my faith into action. I quickly realize that nothing was impossible for me to accomplish.

Still today in my mature adult age I continue to feed and inspire myself through the word of God. Which has caused my inner spirit and mindset to grow stronger. This principle has benefited me in awesome ways. It helps me better myself, enables me to keep a positive attitude and to not give up when life challenges get overwhelming. I've learned the ability to overcome heart ache, defeat and devastating situations. My life has taken on a new meaning, balance and a fulfilled pathway. I started experiencing unexplainable doors of opportunities for financial stability, favor in my career and restoration in my relationships. The list of blessings goes on and on.

I am a living witness and an advocate that the words you release do play a major role in what will manifest into your life and atmosphere. I often think about what would have happen if I had chosen to speak gloom and doom and doubt over my life, my family and situation. I know that I would still be stuck in an unhealthy, going nowhere depressed mess. The damage it would have caused my family would be unbearable. For example, I know some people today all they confess out of their mouth are words of discouragement and no hope for a brighter future, confessing things like:

"I can't"

"I can't afford it"

"I am broke"

"I am sick"

"My life sucks"

"I am never going to find a job"

"I am never going to get out of this situation"

"I am never going to get married"

Some of these same people use words to degrade their children telling them that they are "dumb," "stupid," and "never going to make it in life," "you just like your no-good daddy or momma." The list can go on and on with added profanity. People like this often wonder why themselves and children see no improvement in their life and circumstances. Not understanding using these types of communication can have a boomerang affect that can last for generations. It can lead to depression, self-esteem issues, toxic behavior patterns, despair and poverty which can be hard to overcome. Learning to control our thoughts and tongues is a must. Being careful of the words spoken is important.

The good news is once you know better you do better. It's never too late to change your mindset and communication to become more positive, encouraging and wholesome, which can lead to a successful life for yourself and family. It's a matter of looking at where you are right now and making the decision to change for the better. It doesn't make a difference how old you are, going ahead and finally deciding to do it is a game changer.

I am taking my own advice. In this season of life, I am keeping my mind, heart and words positive and focused to line up with all of Gods promises that he has for me. I cannot let the distractions of this world take me off course with its turmoil and foolishness. I will not allow negativity of my mind or words to drag me down in any type of way. My motto now is " living my life to the fullest." This is my new beginning. Yes, I am speaking it out loud to myself and into the atmosphere. I will finally live my life the way I have dreamed of living. No longer putting off the things I have so desired. Life is too short for procrastination and fear of the unknown.

I want you to join me and lets discover all the wonderful possibilities of enjoying life now. You do not have to settle for less anymore. Regardless of the lies you may have heard or the bad experiences you have encountered. I want to be crystal clear God wants you to succeed in every area of your life. If you will allow him, he will lead and guide you the right way. What God has spoken concerning you in his word is true and not a lie.

Therefore, I wrote this book to help encourage you to dig deep into your mind and heart to uncover any sins, addictions, unforgiveness, hurt, pain, problems and issues that have kept you stuck and bound in chains. I want to help you identify the root causes so the cleansing process can begin. There is an old saying, that says practice makes perfect. The more you repeat and do a thing it will become a habit. I show you how to speak and apply God's faith filled words of truths and promises that will enhance your life.

You must believe that your best days are ahead of you to use your spoken words to decree and declare God's truths and promises over your life. Realize that there is greatness and purpose inside you waiting to be unlocked and explored. Use the power of your words and faith to call into existence things that are not seen yet.

My desire is that your inner spirit will have a renewed strength. That you will have an even greater expectation and determination to accomplish your goals and plans. I invite you for 31 days for 5 minutes or less to start your day with affirmations, meditation scriptures, prayer and reflection questions. This will be the beginning to finally discover the new person that was hidden inside of you. Applying these steppingstones will lead you to the road of healing, wholeness and success.

I celebrate the awesome person you are and all you inspire to be. Now jumpstart your day into your divine destiny and never look back.

Day 1

God Loves Me

I decree and declare these spoken words with confidence, faith and in truth.

I deserve to be loved. My God the father who is the creator of the world loves me. Who or what is greater than that? God your love caused you to give your only son Jesus to die on the cross for my sins to give me eternal life. No person on this earth can ever love me more than that. God your love is anchored deep and is unconditional. No hidden agendas or strings attached. God your love surrounds me 24 hours a day and 7 days a week. You take me as I am through the good, the bad and the ugly things I have done. I am consumed with your love for me. You are the lover of my soul. I am yours and you are mine.

Meditation Scriptures

For God so loved the world, that he gave his only begotten Son, that whosoever believeth in him should not perish, but have everlasting life. – John 3:16 (KJV)

And so, we know and rely on the love God has for us. God is love. Whoever lives in love lives in God, and God in them. – 1 John 4:16 (NIV)

Today's Prayer

Father God I come to you in prayer that you will help me to continue to feel your love and embrace it. I believe in your word that said you are love. Your love is supernatural, always present and forever. Even when I don't feel emotional love, physical love and sometimes when I am incapable of wanting to love others – you know exactly how I am feeling in these vulnerable situations. Help me oh GOD to bring to the surface and remove any unforgiveness I may have hidden deep rooted in my heart against someone so I can love myself and others the way you love me. I thank you that your love is pure and last forever. Help me to express your Godly love daily I pray in Jesus name. Amen.

Reflection:
Write a summary of God's love for you.

_____

_____

_____

_____

_____

Day 2

I Am Fearfully and Wonderfully Made

I decree and declare these spoken words with confidence, faith and in truth.

There is no one on this earth designed like me. I am one of a kind. I am special, unique and hand-picked by God. I love being me and I am like no one else. I am your masterpiece. I am confident in who I am. God I was created in your image and likeness. No one can compare to me. Where I see flaws in myself, you see beauty. You are the potter and I am the clay. I trust you will mold and shape me as you see fit. I will walk with my head held high and not down in shame. I will embrace my awesome design.

Meditation Scriptures

So, God created man in his *own* image, in the image of God created he him; male and female created he them. – Genesis 1:27 (KJV)

For you created my inmost being you knit me together in my mother's womb. I praise you because I am fearfully and wonderfully made; your works are wonderful; I know that full well. – Psalms 139: 13-14 (NIV)

Yet you, LORD, are our Father. We are the clay, you are the potter, we are all the work of your hand. – Isaiah 64:8 (NIV)

Today's Prayer

Father God help me to be proud of who I am in you. It's not about the birth family that I came from. It does not matter what people opinions are about me. I believe in your word that said you created me in your image. Once I decided to accepted Jesus Christ into my life and became spiritually reborn, I now have your DNA in me. God I am crying out to you. Please continue doing your work inside of me and to make me more like you. God, I need you to polish and refine my character from the inside out to shine brighter for all to see. I truly want to represent you in the best way that I can. I pray in Jesus name. Amen.

Reflection:
Write a summary about your uniqueness.

_____

_____

_____

Day 3

I Am Forgiven

I decree and declare these spoken words with confidence, faith and in truth.

I will not speak negative words that mentally beat and tear me down. I will not let others negative words towards me define or condemn me. Jesus died for my past, present and future faults and sins. I will let go of the guilt, pain and shame. No, I am not perfect, and I don't pretend to be. I still make mistakes sometimes. But the moment I repent, God has forgiven me. I must learn how to forgive myself. I will live my life in the goodness of God's grace, mercy and forgiveness.

Meditation Scriptures

In whom we have redemption through his blood, the forgiveness of sins, according to the riches of his grace. – Ephesians 1:7 (KJV)

And their sins and iniquities will I remember no more. – Hebrews 10:17 (KJV)

If we confess our sins, he is faithful and just to forgive us our sins, and to cleanse us from all unrighteousness. – 1 John 1:9 (KJV)

Therefore, there is now no condemnation for those who are in Christ Jesus, because through Christ Jesus the law of the Spirit who gives life has set you free from the law of sin and death. – Romans 8: 1-2 (KJV)

Today's Prayer

Father God, I have an issue when people try to condemn me of my past or present faults. Help me to remember I am forgiven for every evil thought and sin I have committed. I believe in your word that said If I confess and repent of my sins you will forgive me and remember them no more. I am free to live without bondage, baggage and strongholds over me. I break every chain, curse and hindering spirit off me and against me. I pray it is done in Jesus name. Amen.

Reflection:
Write a summary about God's forgiveness.

_____

_____

_____

_____

_____

Day 4

I Am Cleansed

I decree and declare these spoken words with confidence, faith and in truth.

I am cleansed from the inside out. No one can judge what's in my heart but God. God has placed a new mind and heart within me. I have a different outlook and perspective on life. I am a new person. I have removed myself from unclean habits. I will not contaminate myself with negative people and negative environments. My focus is on keeping myself on the positive and wholesome pathway of life.

Meditation Scriptures

Create in me a clean heart, O God; and renew a right spirit within me. – Psalms 51:10 (KJV)

He saved us, not because of righteous things we had done, but because of his mercy. He saved us through the washing of rebirth and renewal by the Holy Spirit. – Titus 3:5 (NIV)

I will cleanse them from all the sin they have committed against me and will forgive all their sins of rebellion against me. – Jeremiah 33:8 (NIV)

You are already clean because of the word I have spoken to you. – John 15:3 (NIV)

Today's Prayer

Father God help me in the struggle to stay cleansed of sin. Some days it's hard not to think, say or do the wrong things. Please keep my mind focused on you. Help me to think before I speak and act. I really want a pure heart and a spirit that is Christ like. I know this will not happen overnight, but it is a lifelong process. Oh God I want a heart to serve you and help others. I want a humble heart and to not be puffed up with self-pride or malice. I want a heart of love, meekness and kindness. I know you will continue to lead and guide me through this transition of cleansing. God I cannot do this by myself. I am asking you to hold my hand and keep me on the straight path in Jesus name. Amen.

Reflection:
Write a summary about your new character.

_____

_____

_____

Day 5

I Am Healed

I decree and declare these spoken words with confidence, faith and in truth.

I am healed in every area of my life. I speak no sickness upon myself. I may not feel like it or look like it now, but I have faith and stand on every healing promise that is given to me in God's word. I speak healing in my atmosphere wherever I may be. I maintain only healthy relationships and not toxic ones. My mind, body and spirit are healthy. I believe the report of the Lord concerning my healing. I release positive energy, wellness and wholeness through every tissue, organ, vein, muscle, bone and flesh in my body internally and externally.

Meditation Scriptures

He sent his word, and healed them, and delivered them from their destructions. – Psalms 107:20 (KJV)

But he was wounded for our transgressions, he was bruised for our iniquities: the chastisement of our peace was upon him; and with his stripes we are healed. – Isaiah 53:5 (KJV)

Beloved, I wish above all things that thou mayest prosper and be in health, even as thy soul prospereth. − 3 John 1:2 (KJV)

Today's Prayer

God increase my faith in your word that declares you are a healer and that I am healed. I believe in your word that said you want me to be healed and to prosper. You sent your word to heal me. Help me realize that I must see my healing in faith before I naturally see it physically or even feel it. I must learn through the pain and suffering that you are with me as you were with Jesus on the cross. You are the true doctor and medicine I need mentally, spiritually or physically. I will not let the devil defeat me in any areas of my healing process. No weapon formed against me shall prosper. I bind and remove every sickness, disease and the spirit of premature death. I will remain strong no matter how I am feeling, you will give me the strength to endure this season in my life. In your word you said God I am in the palms of your hands and no one can pluck me out of them. I claim healing belongs to me right now. Oh God I pray in Jesus name. Amen.

Reflection:
What do you need healing for?

Day 6

I Am Free

I decree and declare these spoken words with confidence, faith and in truth.

Because I am a child of God, I have the choice to repent of my sins. I believe in your word that says by confessing with my mouth and believing in my heart Jesus died and rose from the grave for my sins I am saved. I have accepted Jesus as my Lord and Savior. The greater one's spirit dwells inside of me therefore I am free. No more chains of bondage, sin and addictions can ever hold me captive. I am living in freedom in my mind and spirit. No devil in hell and no devil on this earth has power over me anymore. I celebrate today for Freedom belongs to me.

Meditation Scriptures

Stand fast therefore in the liberty wherewith Christ hath made us free and be not entangled again with the yoke of bondage. – Galatians 5:1 (KJV)

Now the Lord is the Spirit, and where the Spirit of the Lord is, there is freedom. – 2 Corinthians 3:17 (NIV)

But now that you have been set free from sin and have become slaves of God, the benefit you reap leads to holiness, and the result is eternal life. – Romans 6:22 (NIV)

Today's Prayer

Father God help me to have the strength to remain in the freedom you have given me when the devil tries to hold me captive in my mind. I believe in your word that said where the Spirit of the Lord is there is freedom. Oh God I need you to please uphold me when the cravings of addictions or any promiscuous thoughts want to consume me. Please give me the will power to stand and act on your word. Continue to let your saving grace and mercy shower upon me daily. Even through the difficult times of struggle thank you for loving on me and never leaving my side. I understand that my freedom cost you your son's life and I don't take it for granted. You are the strength of my life and all praise and honor is due to you. Keep me close and in your loving arms. I pray in Jesus name Amen.

Reflection:
Write a short summary about your freedom.

_____

_____

Day 7

I Am an Overcomer

I decree and declare these spoken words with confidence, faith and in truth.

Yes, I have been through many ups and downs in my life. Even when my eyes are filled with tears I am still here and standing. I will continue to prevail because your strength is abiding in me. I shall overcome every trial and any circumstances life throws my way. The devil is a liar and I will not be defeated. I will not be overwhelmed with cares of this temporary life for I can conquer anything. I am strong and a warrior. God is my refuge and a strong tower of protection for me.

Meditation Scriptures

You are of God, little children, and have overcome them, because He who is in you is greater than he who is in the world. – 1 John 4:4 (NKJV)

Yet in all these things we are more than conquerors through Him who loved us. – Romans 8:37 (NKJV)

Consider it pure joy, my brothers and sisters, whenever you face trials of many kinds, because you know that the testing of your faith produces perseverance. Let perseverance finish its work so that you may be mature and complete, not lacking anything. – James 1:2–4 (NIV)

Who is it that overcomes the world? Only the one who believes that Jesus is the Son of God. – 1 John 5:5 (NIV)

Today's Prayer

Father God help me to stay focused not on the problems that weigh me down but on you. I believe in your word that said I am more than a conqueror through Him who loved us. When I am weak and exhausted it is you who makes me strong. When I feel like I can't make it another day and can't continue, God it is you who keeps me pressing. When I feel like I am drowning in my sorrow, God it is your spirit that uplifts me to carry on. It is your peace that comforts me. I will prevail no matter what. God all mighty you are my light in the darkness of trouble. I know I am going to make it and there will be victory for me. I pray and it is so in Jesus name Amen.

Reflection:
What have you overcome?

_____

_____

Day 8

I Will Not Fear

I decree and declare these spoken words with confidence, faith and in truth.

I will not worry or fear. No anxiety will fill my mind. I will not have any panic attacks. I will not be nervous or upset. I have a sound mind and it is at rest, peace and in a calm state. This fearful spirit will not paralyze or hold me hostage. I will continue my normal daily functions and activities. I will sleep in peace. I will see my aspirations come to pass. God is with me and is in control of my life. All is well in my soul.

Meditation Scriptures

Peace I leave with you; my peace I give you. I do not give to you as the world gives. Do not let your hearts be troubled and do not be afraid. – John 14:27 (NIV)

The LORD is my light and my salvation— whom shall, I fear? The LORD is the stronghold of my life— of whom shall I be afraid? – Psalms 27:1 (NIV)

O do not fear, for I am with you; do not be dismayed, for I am your God. I will strengthen you and help you; I will uphold you with my righteous right hand. – Isaiah 41:10 (NIV)

For God has not given us a spirit of fear, but of power and of love and of a sound mind. – 2 Timothy 1:7 (NKJV)

Today's Prayer

Father God help me to remain calm and to relax in you. I believe in your word that said I have no reason to fear for you are with me. I ask for your anointing spirit to cast out and remove the spirit of fear that is trying to control my mind. Fear is of the devil and not of you. I will not let strongholds control and paralyze me from becoming successful and walking into my divine destiny and purpose. I ask for your instructions and clarity of mind to lead and guide me on what path I am to travel. I must trust you. When the distractions come before me to bring the spirit of fear, God I shall rebuke it in the power of Jesus name. I shall plead the blood of Jesus against the spirit of fear. God the devil cannot stand your name and must flee at the mention of it. I shall have the courage you have given me. I pray in Jesus name. Amen.

Reflection:
What fear are you releasing today?

Day 9

I Am Strong

I decree and declare these spoken words with confidence, faith and in truth.

I will not break and no one can break my spirit no matter what comes against me. I will not give in and throw in the towel. I can see the chaos all around me but I give it to you God. My feet are planted, I am standing on a solid foundation and I cannot be shaken. I was built strong and not of weakness. God you are my very present help in the times of trouble. I am powerful and I am strong.

Meditation Scriptures

Have I not commanded you? Be strong and courageous. Do not be afraid; do not be discouraged, for the LORD your God will be with you wherever you go. – Joshua 1:9 (NIV)

He gives power to the weak, and to those who have no might He increases strength. – Isaiah 40:29 (NKJV)

Be on your guard; stand firm in the faith; be courageous; be strong. – 1 Corinthians 16:13 (NIV)

The LORD is my rock, my fortress and my deliverer; my God is my rock, in whom I take refuge, my shield and the horn of my salvation, my stronghold. – Psalms 18:2 (NIV)

Today's Prayer

Father God help me endure whatever trouble comes up against me knowing everything is going to be alright. I believe in your word that said be strong in the Lord in your mighty power. Oh God please empower me to be strength for those who are weak and who depend on me. Failure is not an option for me. With you I can't fail. Every day as you grace me to wake up and see a new day, teach me the lessons to persevere as a soldier in combat. God I can face each day with the weapons and armor you have given me. I will stand, fight and win. I will not be intimidated by the devil's schemes and tactics. You are with me pushing me forward. Yes, God it is you who gives me the power that makes me tough. You will not let the devil trample me in defeat. God, I ask please continue to increase my strength daily I pray your will be done in Jesus name. Amen.

Reflection:
Where can you exercise your strength today?

Day 10

I Have the Faith

I decree and declare these spoken words with confidence, faith and in truth.

I believe and trust in you God. Having your divine faith I will not doubt in my ability to succeed. I will not waver in my mind. God you are working all things out for my good. I know I must see the things I am praying and hoping for with my spiritual eyes before I behold them with my natural eyes. In God I move and have my wellbeing. My faith in you God allows great things to happen for me. I expect nothing less when my spirit connects with your spirit. I have earth shaken and mountain moving faith.

Meditation Scriptures

For we live by faith, not by sight. – 2 Corinthians 5:7 (NIV)

But without faith it is impossible to please him: for he that cometh to God must believe that he is, and that he is a rewarder of them that diligently seek him. – Hebrews 11:6 (KJV)

But let him ask in faith, nothing wavering. For he that wavereth is like a wave of the sea driven with the wind and tossed. – James 1:6 (KJV)

And whatever things you ask in prayer, believing, you will receive. – Matthews 21:22 (NKJV)

<u>Today's Prayer</u>

Father God help me increase my faith daily and not to waver in my mind and spirit. I believe in your word that said for we live and walk by faith, not by sight. All I need is a little faith a grain of a mustard seed. To be honest there are areas in my life where my faith is tested. Oh God ease the uncertainty I feel when something is asked of me and I must decide. I want my spirit to connect with you on such a supernatural and deeper level that I have no unrest feelings in my petitions. I know that it is you who hears me and it's you talking to me. I don't have to second guess myself and talk myself out of the promises you have instore for me. God, I ask for more boldness to take the leap of faith where my actions will speak louder than my words. Push me into a higher level of faith, I pray in Jesus name Amen.

Reflection:
In what area can you increase your faith?

_____

Day 11

I Have Grace

I decree and declare these spoken words with confidence, faith and in truth.

By your grace I am saved. Your grace has freed me. I didn't do anything to earn it or deserve it and I cannot take any credit for it. But you have given it to me as a gift and I humbly accept it and I am truly grateful. Daily your supernatural grace surrounds me, carries me and restores me to my rightful place in you God. I embrace my life's path with love, joy, peace, courage and dignity. I will graciously tackle any task or problems that arises with wisdom for a positive outcome. For whatever decision I need to make or goals I need to accomplish your gracious spirit is there to guide me.

Meditation Scriptures

For by grace are ye saved through faith; and that not of yourselves: it is the gift of God: Not of works, lest any man should boast.
– Ephesian 2:8-9 (KJV)

Let us then approach God's throne of grace with confidence, so that we may receive mercy and find grace to help us in our time of need.
– Hebrews 4:16 (NIV)

For sin shall not have dominion over you: for ye are not under the law, but under grace.
– Romans 6:14 (KJV)

He has saved us and called us to a holy life not because of anything we have done but because of his own purpose and grace. This grace was given us in Christ Jesus before the beginning of time. – 2 Timothy 1:9 (NIV)

Today's Prayer

Father God help me to live, talk and walk in your grace daily. I believe in your word that said I am not under the law of sin, but under grace. I can come to you and find grace to help me in times of need and despair. Teach me to demonstrate your grace to others. Please keep your hand upon me so my grace will never run out. I never want to sin against you. Help me to have pure thoughts in words, deeds and actions. Continue to manifest your grace generously upon me. I want to be pleasing in your sight. May I stay in your will that your grace will lead and guide me in the right direction. Please keep the outpouring of favor and blessings flowing in my life. I pray in Jesus name. Amen.

Reflection:
Write a summary about God's grace.

_____

_____

_____

_____

_____

_____

_____

_____

_____

_____

_____

_____

Day 12

I Have Mercy

I decree and declare these spoken words with confidence, faith and in truth.

God is merciful to me. God's mercy towards me is forever. I know I don't always do everything right. I really deserve punishment for the ungodly actions and mistakes I have committed repeatedly. God you could have written me off a long time ago but you did not. Instead your tender mercies, great faithfulness, loving kindness and compassion are towards me every day. I thank you for your patience with me while I am going through theses ever changing seasons in my life.

Meditation Scriptures

It is of the LORD's mercies that we are not consumed, because his compassions fail not. They are new every morning: great is thy faithfulness. − Lamentations 3:22-23 (KJV)

The LORD is gracious, and full of compassion; slow to anger, and of great mercy. The LORD is good to all: and his tender mercies are over all his works. − Psalms 145:8-9 (KJV)

Who is a God like you, who pardons sin and forgives the transgression of the remnant of his
40

inheritance? You do not stay angry forever but delight to show mercy. – Micah 7:18 (NIV)

<u>Today's Prayer</u>

Father God it is so hard for me but help me to truly have a heart of mercy toward others even when it is difficult. I believe in your word that said mercies are new every morning. God may your divine tender mercies rain fresh as dew each morning. I never want to forget the mercy you have shown me throughout my life. I ask you to continue to have mercy and forgive the wrong doings that I have committed and may do in the future. Sometimes my inner weakness overcomes me. God you already know I am imperfect with many flaws. I ask that you never let your love run out for me. Oh God I ask you to sustain me in your loving care forever. Daily I will give you the honor and glory. Yes, I pray this in Jesus name. Amen.

Reflection:
Write a summary about God's mercy towards you.

_____

_____

Day 13

I Am Protected

I decree and declare these spoken words with confidence, faith and in truth.

God your hand and protection is always upon me. I plead the shed blood of Jesus as protection over me. I will not allow my mouth, eyes and ear gates to be unprotected by the pollution of negativity and sin. My relationships are guarded and safe from the enemy's tactics and schemes. I am secure in my dwelling place, my properties, my school, my church, my travels, my corporate business and work environment are all secure in you. God, I believe that you already have my future covered. No weapons of evil that is formed against me shall prosper. God your heavenly angels are dispatched to watch, surround and protect me 24 hours a day and 7 days a week.

Meditation Scriptures

Though I walk during trouble, thou wilt revive me: thou shalt stretch forth thine hand against the wrath of mine enemies, and thy right hand shall save me. − Psalms 138:7 (KJV)

For he shall give his angels charge over thee, to keep thee in all thy ways. − Psalms 91:11 (KJV)

42

But the Lord is faithful, and he will strengthen you and protect you from the evil one. – 2 Thessalonians 3:3 (NIV)

Father God continue to protect me daily. I believe in your word that said you shall give your angels charge over me. God, I pray I will not suffer harm for you are with me. I ask for your defense against the unknown. Guard me as a shield. God, I plead the shed blood of Jesus over me. As I travel and even while I am asleep, Oh God I pray that you cover me. You know the devil seeks to kill and destroy me and my family. God you are my hiding place where I can run and find safety. Danger is across the land and the devil's attacks are violent, but I will not worry. I know you will deliver me because you keep a watchful eye on the evil one. God, I rest and depend on you eternal God for my safety. In faith in Jesus name I pray. Amen.

Reflection:
Write a summary to define God's protection.

_____

_____

Day 14
I Am Victorious

I decree and declare these spoken words with confidence, faith and in truth.

I will not listen to the devil's lies. I am not a loser. I will never be defeated. With God's help I will win in whatever I set my mind to. Giving up is not an option for me. I have faith in God, trusting that all things are possible for those who believe and trust in him. I know that the greater one that lives inside of me is pushing me to excel to the next level. I am a child of God. I read, I meditate, and I apply the word of God into every area of my life. According to the words of God in the scriptures I have inherited promises and blessings. All things are working in my favor mentally, spiritually, physically and financially. Victory belongs to me now and forever.

Meditation Scriptures

For the LORD your God is the one who goes with you to fight for you against your enemies to give you victory. – Deuteronomy 20:4 (NIV)

But thanks be to God! He gives us the victory through our Lord Jesus Christ. – 1 Corinthians 15:57 (NIV)

And we know that all things work together for good to those who love God, to those who are the called according to His purpose. – Romans 8:28 (NKJV)

Today's Prayer

Father God help me when I feel emotionally down in spirit to believe in your word that said victory belongs to me through our Lord Jesus Christ. I know the devil's job is to bring a spirit of discouragement. But I come against it with the power that is instilled inside me. God keep me focused on the champion that I am. Keep me grounded and help me not to forget it's you who has given me the mindset and power to win. God my desire is to be in the center of your will, understanding no victories can be accomplished by myself. Without you I will fall flat on my face and fail. Eternal God I ask you to keep your spirit within me so I will be inspired and motivated to see continued victories throughout my life. I pray with confidence in Jesus name. Amen.

Reflection:
Write a summary on what it means to be victorious.

_____

_____

Day 15

Nobody Can Stop Me

I decree and declare these spoken words with confidence, faith and in truth.

The devil cannot hinder or stop my progress. I will not be lazy, passive and procrastinate in executing my dreams, plans and goals. I will write down my vision which will be plainly seen and known in the earth. I am focused on what I want, what I so desire and what I deserve. I am a go getter and I am unstoppable. I will not be distracted by the bumps and pitfalls in the road. I am a champion and I see the prize ahead of me and I am going for it all with God's help.

Meditation Scriptures

I can do all things through Christ who strengthens me. − Philippians 4:13 (NKJV)

Let us not become weary in doing good, for at the proper time we will reap a harvest if we do not give up. − Galatians 6:9 (NIV)

Do you know in a race all the runners run, but only one gets the prize? Run in such a way as to get the prize. − 1 Corinthians 9:24 (NIV)

Today's Prayer

Father God see my heart, help me not to get tired and quit in my well doing. My harvest of blessings will be great and not just in the afterlife but right here on earth. The devil doesn't want to see me blessed. I cannot stop because of oppositions and naysayers. Oh God let the fire continue to burn in my soul to always be a Godly example, to have positive and inspiring conversations with all people in the world. To lend a helping hand to assist those in need. Please God help me to keep running in this race called life. I will not stop in my tracks but will keep on going. God, I know the rewards will be great. God just help me to hang on in there to see what you have in store for me. I am trusting and praying in Jesus name. Amen.

Reflection:
Write a summary of why you are unstoppable.

_____

_____

_____

_____

Day 16

Power in My Words

I decree and declare these spoken words with confidence, faith and in truth.

My words are powerful and they create whatever I release into the atmosphere. I must guard the words that come out of my mouth. I will speak life and not death over myself and future. I will not bring a curse or negative energy on myself, family and future. I release words of faith, healing, blessings and success. I will speak words in a calm tone that are positive, that will inspire and give encouragement to others. I will not speak condemnation, judgment, gossip or evilness to myself or others. With my words I will be able to change doubt into faith. I am a Godly seed sower.

Meditation Scriptures

The tongue has the power of life and death, and those who love it will eat its fruit. – Proverbs 18:21 (NIV)

Out of the same mouth proceeded blessing and cursing. My brethren, these things ought not so to be. – James 3:10 (KJV)

The soothing tongue is a tree of life, but a perverse tongue crushes the spirit. – Proverbs 15:4 (NIV)

Today's Prayer

Father God help me to think about the tone and words I will speak before they are released. Clean my heart from any negativity and evil. In your word it says out of the heart the mouth speaks. Because once the words go out in the atmosphere, I cannot take them back. I do not want to cause hurt and harm to anyone. Even in a disagreement let my words be understood in a calm matter. God please anoint my tongue to praise, worship and give you thanks. God let me speak forth blessings upon my future and family and not a curse. Let the words of my mouth and the meditation of my heart be acceptable in your sight, O Lord, my strength and redeemer I pray in Jesus name. Amen.

Reflection:
Write a summary about using your words.

_____

_____

_____

Day 17

I Look Good

I decree and declare these spoken words with confidence, faith and in truth.

God your divine favor is upon me and it looks good on me. Your presence radiates through me. My glow illuminates from the inside out for the world to see. I have high self-esteem with my head held high, my walk is upright and with every step I will not stumble. It's not arrogance or a prideful heart or attitude. It's the God that is within me. I am wearing you well in my every day and my professional life. Beauty is said to be in the eyes of the beholder. People are attracted to me because of who you are in my life. I am God's gift to those who you have placed in my life. I make a huge difference and impact on others. I am an example and have the characteristics of being God's child.

Meditation Scripture

And let the beauty of the LORD our God be upon us and establish the work of our hands for us; Yes, establish the work of our hands.
– Psalms 90:17 (NKJV)

Surely, LORD, you bless the righteous you surround them with your favor as with a shield.
– Psalms 5:12 (NIV)

And so, find favor and high esteem in the sight of God and man. – Proverbs 3:4 (NKJV)

Today's Prayer

Father God I believe your word when it said you will bless the righteous and establish our ways. I will have favor with you and man. God I never want to think more highly of myself out of pride. Keep me rooted in you and never let me get too far removed out of your will. Oh, Eternal God continue to let your glory illuminate through me that others will want to know what it is that draws people to connect with me. Please use this as an opportunity for me to witness to others. God instruct me to show others how they can experience your awesome spirit, love, freedom, deliverance, healing and all you have to offer in their life. Always keep my mind in the will and center of you God. Always keep me spiritually alert and physically healthy. Divine God I pray in Jesus name. Amen.

Reflection:
Pick one scripture to encourage yourself.

Day 18

I Am Blessed

I decree and declare these spoken words with confidence, faith and in truth.

God, I receive and will maintain all the promised blessings you have for me. I am the heir of your kingdom and I have the rights to it. I will live my life in the overflow of blessings. Not just in the natural of material possessions but in the spiritual ones as well. God's glory shines upon me. Anything I set my mind and hands to do I produce fruitful results. God commands wonderous things to happen for me. I thank you God for your provisions. I thank you that you cause people to show me favor. I have such an abundance of wealth that I am returning the blessing to others. I do not take anything I have or what you do for me for granted.

Meditation Scriptures

And it shall come to pass, if thou shalt hearken diligently unto the voice of the Lord thy God, to observe and to do all his commandments which I command thee this day, that the Lord thy God will set thee on high above all nations of the earth: And all these blessings shall come on thee, and overtake thee, if thou shalt hearken unto the voice of the Lord thy God.

Blessed shalt thou be in the city, and blessed shalt thou be in the field. Blessed shall be the fruit of thy body, and the fruit of thy ground, and the fruit of thy cattle, the increase of thy kind, and the flocks of thy sheep. Blessed shall be thy basket and thy store. Blessed shalt thou be when thou comest in, and Blessed shalt thou be when thou goest out.

The LORD shall command the blessing upon thee in thy storehouses, and in all that thou settest thine hand unto; and he shall bless thee in the land which the LORD thy God giveth thee.

And the LORD shall make thee plenteous in goods, in the fruit of thy body, and in the fruit of thy cattle, and in the fruit of thy ground, in the land which the LORD swore unto thy fathers to give thee.

The LORD shall open unto thee his good treasure, the heaven to give the rain unto thy land in his season, and to bless all the work of thine hand: and thou shalt lend unto many nations, and thou shalt not borrow.

And the LORD shall make thee the head, and not the tail; and thou shalt be above only, and thou shalt not be beneath; if that thou hearken unto the commandments of the LORD thy God, which I command thee this day, to observe and to do them. – Deuteronomy 28: 1 – 6, 8, 11–13 (KJV)

<u>Today's Prayer</u>

God continue to help me understand that it is not my job, education or professional circle that makes me blessed. Father God you are my source which allows me to get access to resources. I don't have to settle for nothing less than what you have for me. Your word says if I seek you first then everything else will be added unto me. I am rich in your abundance. God your word says if I keep your commandments and I abide in you I am blessed and highly favored. God its only you who will open the windows of heaven and pour me out blessings that I won't have room enough to receive. Holy God please let me experience every blessing that you have for me known and even the ones that are unknown. Bless me with a long healthy life to see it all. In expectance I pray in Jesus name. Amen.

Reflection:
Write a summary on how you are blessed.

_____

_____

_____

_____

Day 19
It's What God Say's About Me

I decree and declare these spoken words with confidence, faith and in truth.

I will not be disturbed or upset by the negative looks, words or thoughts people may say about me. I belong to God and it is what he says about me that matters. I know who I am in him. I am royalty and priceless and I will not settle for anything less. I am not ashamed of who I am or what I have been through. God is the potter and I am the clay. He is shaping and molding me. I am a vessel being used by God. I am a living testimony for the world to see.

Meditation Scriptures

But you are a chosen people, a royal priesthood, a holy nation, God's special possession, that you may declare the praises of him who called you out of darkness into his wonderful light. − 1 Peter 2:9 (NIV)

See what great love the Father has lavished on us, that we should be called children of God! And that is what we are! The reason the world does not know us is that it did not know him. − 1 John 3:1 (NIV)

For you are a holy people to the LORD your God, and the LORD has chosen you to be a people for Himself, a special treasure above all the peoples who are on the face of the earth.
– Deuteronomy 14:2 (NKJV)

Today's Prayer

Father God I really need you now. Help me not be focused on the naysayers and the untruths of people's words. I believe your word when it said I am called the children of God. Heavenly Father I believe your word said I am chosen and a royal priesthood and a special treasure. I have become a new person in you. The devil likes to degrade me. He always wants to bring up my past mistakes and failures. God help me to remember I am chosen by you. God help me to block, stop listening and reading the gossip and the defaming on the social media outlets that talk about me. Give me the inner strength to turn away from the world's negative views and to continue to read and pray your words of truth as a foundation to lean and stand firm on. I am standing in your will, ways and truth. I pray this in your son Jesus name. Amen.

Reflection:
Who does God say you are?

Day 20

I Love Myself

I decree and declare these spoken words with confidence, faith and in truth.

I have many shortcomings but by knowing the divine love you have for me God. I choose to love myself and not hate. I will not bring mental or physical harm to myself. I will not accept anyone else's verbal, mental or physical abuse. I am not insecure but confident. I love, cherish and respect myself. I am proud of the way God made me. I am beautiful or handsome and any make overs will be done God's way. I am creative, smart and intelligent. I do not need anyone else's validation but yours God. I am not defined by my past mistakes or who I used to be. The love that I have the world did not give it to me and the world cannot take it away.

Meditation Scriptures

After all, no one ever hated their own body, but they feed and care for their body, just as Christ does the church. – Ephesians 5:29 (NIV)

Do you not know that your bodies are temples of the Holy Spirit, who is in you, whom you have received from God? You are not your own; you were bought at a price. Therefore, honor God with your bodies. −1 Corinthians 6:19−20 (NIV)

Therefore, if anyone is in Christ, he is a new creation; old things have passed away; behold, all things have become new. − 2 Corinthians 5:17 (NKJV)

Today's Prayer

God help me to realize that I need to love myself more and not focus on my faults, failures and my physical genetic design. Help me not to have self −hatred but a genuine love for myself and others. I need the will power to maintain my body. I believe your word that said my body is a holy temple. When I get off track help me to care for my body spiritually, mentally and physically. Help me to be mindful of the negative visible and audible things that can filter into my body. O God give me the will power and energy to keep myself healthy and whole. Most important may my focus be on strengthening my inner spirit so I can build a closer relationship with you and others through love. I pray in Jesus name. Amen.

Reflection:
Write one thing you love about yourself.

Day 21

I Am Encouraged

I decree and declare these spoken words with confidence, faith and in truth.

This will be an awesome day. I am changing everyday becoming a better me. Things are looking up and getting much better for me. God is almighty in my life. God can do exceedingly abundantly above what I can ask or imagination. Everything I desire shall be granted. I will experience life changing miracles. God has me in the palm of his hands and no one will take me out of them. God will care for and sustain me all the days of my life. I will dwell in everlasting peace and success.

Meditation Scriptures

Even to your old age and gray hairs I am he, I am he who will sustain you. I have made you and I will carry you: I will sustain you and I will rescue you.
– Isaiah 46:4 (NIV)

For with God nothing shall be impossible with God. – Luke 1:37 (KJV)

These things I have spoken to you, that in Me you may have peace. In the world you will have tribulation; but be of good cheer, I have overcome the world. – John 16:33 (NKJV)

Today's Prayer

Father God help me to learn to encourage myself in your word during these trying times of uncertainty. I believe your word said you are with me and you will uphold me and never forsake me. Help me to fill my mind with all the wonderous things you have done for me and what is in store for my future. When I think about your goodness to me and my family my soul shouts hallelujah. God sometimes I may feel overwhelmed but still awesome God my soul will rest in you and not in the abilities of natural man. God you are the lifter of my soul. God no matter what the circumstances I pray I can still laugh, dance and sing in the rain. When I seek you God I am energized to keep pushing ahead. You are the reason I keep my head above water without sinking in despair. Oh God you are my hope and serenity. Keep me dear and near to you. I pray in Jesus name. Amen.

Reflection:
Write a summary to encourage yourself.

_____

_____

Day 22
I Lack No Good Thing

I decree and declare these spoken words with confidence, faith and in truth.

I shall not have any lack in my life. I will no longer have to struggle just trying to make it or get by. I will not have the spirit of "I can't" or "I can't have." I will not be broke, poor and disgusted in my spirit. I will not settle for less. I will not live a life of mediocrity. I shall have more than enough running over in abundance. It's my time to knock down the barriers in my mind and thrust into my moment of opportunities and greatness. I seek God first for directions and timing. I am driven, motivated and ready to start the process. I am willing and able to do what is necessary to claim and grab hold of what is mines.

Meditation Scripture

For the LORD God is a sun and shield:
the LORD will give grace and glory: no good thing will he withhold from them that walk uprightly. – Psalms 84:11 (KJV)

But seek first his kingdom and his righteousness, and all these things will be given to you as well.
– Matthew 6:33 (NIV)

Give, and it will be given to you. A good measure, pressed down, shaken together and running over, will be poured into your lap. For with the measure you use, it will be measured to you. – Luke 6:38 (NIV)

Today's Prayer

Father God keep my mind off the thought of losing everything I have worked for and gained. Please help me to trust you at your word completely regarding your rewarding benefits to me. Your word said to seek first your kingdom and righteousness, to obey you and follow your commands that the blessings will overtake me. God you said in your word you never seen the righteous person or their seed begging for bread. You are my and my families provider. I bind the spirit of lack and poverty. I release blessings upon blessing for me and my family in Jesus name. Oh God I pray my mind will learn and comprehend all the wisdom and knowledge that you have available for me. God prepare me and increase my skill set so I can be equipped for the journey that is before me. Wonderful God I pray you will intentionally be generous to me throughout my lifetime. I am keeping the faith until the end in Jesus name. Amen.

Reflection:
Write an affirmation about lacking nothing.

_____

_____

_____

_____

_____

_____

_____

_____

_____

_____

_____

Day 23

My Purpose Is Great

I decree and declare these spoken words with confidence, faith and in truth.

The greater one lives inside of me pushing me to excel beyond what I can see. I feel the passion burning in my soul and the tugging in my spirit. My natural birth here on earth was not by accident or a mistake. I am called to something bigger than I can even imagine. My gifts, talents and ability to connect with influential people was all designed by God. The right doors will open for me to walk through and the wrong doors will remain closed. I learned that the roadblocks of mishaps in my life are teaching tools for my advancement on what's next to come. I must stay grounded, levelheaded and focused on my assignment.

Meditation Scriptures

For it is God who works in you to will and to act in order to fulfill his good purpose. – Philippians 2:13 (NIV)

Many are the plans in a person's heart, but it is the LORD's purpose that prevails. – Proverbs 19:21 (NIV)

For I know the plans I have for you," declares the LORD, "plans to prosper you and not to harm you, plans to give you hope and a future.
– Jeremiah 29:11 (NIV)

Today's Prayer

Father God I ask you to give me the tenacity to achieve my purpose. In the face of adversity help me to have fortitude to keep on going. I know you intentionally have me here for a reason and for a great purpose. I don't want to go ahead of you with my own mission and prideful hidden agenda. Please manifest clearly the assignment I am to fulfill. God help me to sit still, pray and listen to your voice. I need the blueprint to lead me to the destination in the right season. Give me the discernment to be aware of business ventures and professional dealings that I must undertake. God let any platform that I am on be used as an avenue to release the purpose you have for me. I pray in Jesus name. Amen

Reflection:
Write a summary on what your purpose is.

_____

_____

Day 24

I Will Not Be Depressed

I decree and declare these spoken words with confidence, faith and in truth.

The battle of depression is in my mind and I will take control of it in order to survive. I will not feel confused, sad, be in a bad mood, feel loneliness or have suicidal thoughts. In time I know my grief, sickness and personal problems will soon fade. I will not let this evil spirit consume me. I will not be held a prisoner in my own mind. I will replace these negative thoughts in my head daily with prayer, counseling, positive meditation and reading the words of God. There is no shame in seeking professional care. God uses doctors and therapist here on earth to help my mental and physical needs. I will get through anything with God's help. I will walk in my new beginning to explore the destiny that awaits me.

Meditation Scriptures

Cast all your anxiety on him because he cares for you. – 1 Peter 5:7 (NIV)

Finally, brothers and sisters, whatever is true, whatever is noble, whatever is right, whatever is pure, whatever is lovely, whatever is admirable—if anything is excellent or

praiseworthy—think about such things. –
Philippians 4:8 (NIV)

The LORD is a refuge for the oppressed, a
stronghold in times of trouble. – Psalms 9:9
(NIV)

<u>Today's Prayer</u>

Father God heal me from all negative mental
emotions. I believe your word said you will
keep me in perfect peace when my mind is
stayed on you. You are my refuge for any
oppression or depression. God you are the one
who formed and developed my mind. Holy God I
ask you to remove the clutter, the emptiness
and the disturbances that plague it. The devil
doesn't want me to think right. He wants me to
make unwise decisions and have destructive
thoughts that will cause harm. He is the cause
of this deep dark spirit that is over me. Please
restore my sanity with a touch of your divine
healing. Divine God break this demonic mental
disorder from me now. I pull down every
thought or imagination captive in my mind that
is not pleasing to you. My mind will obey the
voice of the true and living God. It is so I pray
in Jesus name. Amen.

Reflection:
What situation do you need to give to God?

Day 25
I Will Not Stress

I decree and declare these spoken words with confidence, faith and in truth.

Breathing Exercise: Inhale and exhale. Again, inhale and exhale. One more time, inhale and exhale.

I will not allow stress to invade my inner thoughts, bring sickness to my body or surroundings. God when I feel the tension and the anxiety up rising, I will immediately give it over to you. No pressures of life will overwhelm me. When I face constant conflicting issues, I will allow God to resolve them. I will not be frustrated or shaken. The battle is not mine to fight but belongs to God. I will be in perfect harmony with myself and others.

Meditation Scriptures

Cast your cares on the LORD and he will sustain you; he will never let the righteous be shaken.
– Psalms 55:22 (NIV)

Do not be anxious about anything, but in every situation, by prayer and petition, with thanksgiving, present your requests to God. And the peace of God, which transcends

all understanding, will guard your hearts and your minds in Christ Jesus.
– Philippians 4:6-7 (NIV)

And do not be conformed to this world, but be transformed by the renewing of your mind, that you may prove what *is* that good and acceptable and perfect will of God. – Romans 12:2 (NKJV)

Today's Prayer

Father God help me to learn how to be stress free and to depend more on you to handle my problems. I believe your word when it says not to be anxious about anything, to give you my cares and your spirit will give me a life of peace during troubled times. I know living everyday stress free will be a challenge and will not be easy. God, I know that if I stay in your presence and rooted in your word, I can master any task with a calm spirit and balance. As I lay down to sleep give me a peaceful and restful night. Help me not to ponder and toss all night thinking about tomorrows problems. God let your assurance cover me to lean and depend on you. God you know what's best for me. You said you will not give me more than I can carry. God in my daily routine help me to remember that. Praying all these requests in Jesus name. Amen.

Reflection:
Write a summary on stress relief techniques.

_____

_____

_____

_____

_____

_____

_____

_____

_____

_____

_____

Day 26

I Will Not Be Bitter

I decree and declare these spoken words with confidence, faith and in truth.

I will remove all hatred and malice out of my heart. I must let go of all jealously and strife. I will not let anger and rage consume my thoughts. For what's in my heart, my mouth will speak, and it will show in my actions. I cannot concern myself with the foolishness of others. I will be kind, polite and understanding of others. I must be the better person in any situation. I must move forward in my divine path of life.

Meditation Scriptures

Get rid of all bitterness, rage and anger, brawling and slander, along with every form of malice. Be kind and compassionate to one another, forgiving each other, just as in Christ God forgave you.
– Ephesians 4:31–32 (NIV)

Do not take revenge, my dear friends, but leave room for God's wrath, for it is written: "It is mine to avenge; I will repay," says the Lord. – Romans 12:19 (NIV)

And when you stand praying, if you hold anything against anyone, forgive them, so that your Father in heaven may forgive you your sins. – Mark 11:25 (NIV)

So, watch yourselves. "If your brother or sister sins against you, rebuke them; and if they repent, forgive them. Even if they sin against you seven times in a day and seven times come back to you saying, 'I repent,' you must forgive them. – Luke 17:3-4 (NIV)

Today's Prayer

Father God, I repent of bitterness I let live on in my heart please remove this sin from me. I believe that if I hold anything against someone, I really need to forgive them quick, and you will forgive me of my sins. God help me not to be easily offended by what people say or do. Give me the power to ignore offense and to be in goodwill with others. God help me to be sensitive in my communication and behaviors. I do not want my words to be harmful to anyone. I do not want to give anyone a cause to have ill feelings towards me. I do not want to have a do evil for evil mentally. God, I do not want you to withhold blessings from me due to unforgiveness. Whatever wrath is within me, kill it out now. I want to have a good conscience and a bright and lucrative future. I pray in Jesus name. Amen.

Reflection:
Write a summary on letting go of bitterness.

_____

_____

_____

_____

_____

_____

_____

_____

_____

_____

_____

_____

Day 27

I Will Not Be Envious

I decree and declare these spoken words with confidence, faith and in truth.

I will not covet what others may have. I will not compare myself and life to others. I shall not be jealous of people's careers, skills, talents, relationships and possessions. I will not hold resentment towards others. I will not portray hostility toward others. I will encourage, support and be happy for other's success.

Meditation Scriptures

For where envying and strife is, there is confusion and every evil work. – James 3:16 (KJV)

Be not overcome of evil but overcome evil with good. – Romans 12:21 (KJV)

Love is patient, love is kind. It does not envy, it does not boast, it is not proud. It does not dishonor others, it is not self-seeking, it is not easily angered, it keeps no record of wrongs. Love does not delight in evil but rejoices with the truth.
– 1 Corinthians 13:4-6 (NIV)

Today's Prayer

Father God deliver me from envy, covetness and jealous spirits. Help me not to be frustrated when I see or hear about others being blessed. God help me to have the common sense to know you also reward others with good gifts too. I cannot be selfless and resentful. You said in your word you rain on the just as well as the unjust. I cannot judge or justify how or why you are good to others. God when I take my eyes off you and get off track remind me to have a grateful and thankful spirit. I must appreciate you for all you have done for me and my family and what you will continue to do. God help me to have a loving spirit with no evil hidden motives attached. Eternal God help me to do good towards all others. I pray this with a humble heart in Jesus name. Amen

Reflection:
Write a summary on being free of envy.

_____

_____

_____

_____

_____

Day 28

I Will Have Patience

I decree and declare these spoken words with confidence, faith and in truth.

God hears my prayer request. I will wait patiently on God's timing even through my pain and suffering. I will not become upset and have a complaining spirit. God knows how to heal, deliver, restore and bless me. I know sometimes a prayer delayed is not a prayer denied. I shall not get tired and stop believing on God's promises now and those to come. My breakthrough is coming. I am one step closer to my miracles than I was yesterday. I have the fruit of the spirit − long suffering. I can deal with the waiting process. Good things are coming to me because I am patient. As I continue going about my day I will be still in spirit and wait on God. I will maintain my joy and keep smiling while I wait.

Meditation Scriptures

But as for you, be strong and do not give up, for your work will be rewarded. − 2 Chronicles 15:7 (NIV)

Be joyful in hope, patient in affliction, faithful in prayer. − Romans 12:12 (NIV)

I waited patiently for the LORD; he turned to me and heard my cry. – Psalms 40:1 (NIV)

Today's Prayer

Father God help me to be patient and continue in prayer. I believe your word said for me not to grow weary while doing well and my due season will come if I don't give up. Sometimes I feel like life is passing me by. It appears I have been praying and waiting for answered prayers for along time. But God if it's any sin that is blocking or causing a delay, please reveal it to me so I can confess it and repent of it immediately. Oh God please slow me down, so I am not in a hurry to try and make things happen for myself. God as I wait let your glory fill my soul so I can remain steadfast and unmovable. God I will continue giving you the praises while I wait on you. God I am sure your timing is best. Please keep me in perfect peace during the process. I pray in Jesus name. Amen.

Reflection:
Write a summary on the meaning of patience.

_____

_____

_____

Day 29

My Goals and Plans Will Happen

I decree and declare these spoken words with confidence, faith and in truth.

I put my faith and trust in God, for you are my anchor and confidant. With you God by my side all things are possible for me. I have the wisdom, discipline, passion, courage, stamina and the ability to achieve my dreams, visions, goals and plans. I know that amazing business, partnership and entrepreneurship opportunities will happen for me. God you will give me creative ideas in my career on how to secure financial wealth for a lifetime. I speak divine connections and platforms. God will enlarge my territory around the world. My divine destiny will be life-changing for myself, family and a benefit for others who are associated to me.

Meditation Scriptures

If you believe, you will receive whatever you ask for in prayer. - Matthews 21:22 (NIV)

Now faith is confidence in what we hope for and assurance about what we do not see. - Hebrews 11:1 (NIV)

May he give you the desire of your heart and make all your plans succeed. – Psalms 20:4 (NIV)

And the LORD answered me, and said, Write the vision, and make it plain upon tables, that he may run that readeth it. For the vision is yet for an appointed time, but at the end it shall speak, and not lie though it tarry, wait for it; because it will surely come, it will not tarry. – Habakkuk 2: 2-3 (KJV)

Today's Prayer

God help me continue to aim high to reach my desired goals. Free my mind from doubting my vision. Your word said I am the head and not the tail. I am above and not beneath. God you want me to succeed. I have prayed and given you my ideas and plans for consultation and answers. I can only achieve success if I seek you and stay in your divine will. Father God I am willing to make any necessary changes of improvement that need to be done on my part. God whatever problems arise along the journey I know you will solve. God you will guide me on how to turn every negative situation into a positive one. The road may be tough, but I believe getting to the end will be worth the awesome reward. My hope is in you I pray this in Jesus name. Amen.

Reflection:
Write a summary about your goals and plans.

_____

_____

_____

_____

_____

_____

_____

_____

_____

_____

_____

_____

_____

Day 30
I Will Stay Focused

I decree and declare these spoken words with confidence, faith and in truth.

I will focus and concentrate on the word of God day and night. My steps are ordered and guided by God. I will not focus on the devil's schemes and plots. I already have a plan for the enemies wicked devices. I embrace your spirit God to keep me on the right track. I look to you God to help keep me in balance and tranquility. I will have stability in my life. I will focus on wellness and good health for my mental, spiritual and physical wellbeing. I will be committed to the end. My purpose will be fulfilled.

Meditation Scriptures

Order my steps in thy word: and let not any iniquity have dominion over me. − Psalms 119:133 (KJV)

Set your minds on things above, not on earthly things. − Colossians 3:2 (NIV)

Let your eyes look straight ahead, and your eyelids look right before you. − Proverbs 4:25 (NKJV)

Today's Prayer

God help me not to be distracted by people or circumstances. I want to lean and depend only on you. Keep me working diligently on my projects, goals and plans. Help me to balance my daily schedule so I can invest more quality time preparing for my future. Help me pay attention to the resources that are around me to accelerate my financial growth. God, increase my memory so I will not forget people, places or things that are to be beneficial to my success. Help me to never forget and thank all the people that gave me any type of assistance along the way. God, I request divine wisdom, strength and durability to stay focus for all the great assignment now and in the future. I pray in Jesus name. Amen

Reflection:
Write a summary about staying focused.

_____

_____

_____

_____

_____

Day 31

I Will Be Happy

I decree and declare these spoken words with confidence, faith and in truth.

I choose to be happy, satisfied, and content. I rejoice in you God always. I create a happy environment wherever I go. My joy brings happiness to people around me. I inspire people to better themselves. I will have an upbeat and enthusiastic attitude when dealing with the chaos of life's ups and downs. I refuse to let anything, or anyone bring me down and break my spirit. God is totally within me. I am a living example of the true love and joy only God can give me.

Meditation Scriptures

But may the righteous be glad and rejoice before God; may they be happy and joyful. – Psalms 68:3 (NIV)

I have told you this so that my joy may be in you and that your joy may be complete. – John 15:11 (NIV)

I keep my eyes always on the LORD. With him at my right hand, I will not be shaken. Therefore, my heart is glad, and my tongue rejoices; my

body also will rest secure. – Psalms 16:8-9
(NIV)

You make known to me the path of life; you will
fill me with joy in your presence, with eternal
pleasures at your right hand. – Psalms 16:11
(NIV)

<u>Today's Prayer</u>

Father God help me to display your happiness
and joy to the world. Your word said your joy
gives me strength. Happy are the people who
trust in you and not in man. God you know at
certain times when all hell is breaking out in my
life, I start feeling the spirit of sadness.
Sometimes I admit in my weakness I fall back in
my old way of thinking and familiar unhealthy
habits. Oh God help me understand that true
happiness is not found in my own wisdom,
career, money, material items, people,
affection, sex, drugs, alcohol or overeating.

Help me get through the bad times when
they come upon me. Please God wrap me in
your arms, wipe my tears and take the pain
away. Help me remember that troubles do not
last always and joy will come again. God, I
know the void, the sadness and pain I
experience is due to missed quality time with
you. God I am sorry let's get together again.
Please God let your happiness fill me up again,
that my days will be restored with joy

everlasting more than it was before. Being successful should be a happy journey and not a sad one. God I am yours and my future is meant to be filled with love, hope, peace, joy and happiness. It shall be I pray in Jesus name. Amen

Reflection:
Summarize your happiness in one word.

_____

JUMP START

Congratulations! You have completed your 31 days of speaking affirmations, praying and reading meditation scriptures. You can start over again the next month reading the book as many times as you desire to get your breakthrough and see results.

By now you should feel encouraged, inspired and mentally, spiritually and physically stronger. You should be ready to continue your journey to your destiny. You should start to see physical changes manifest from your spoken word and spending time with God. If you haven yet, keep speaking your affirmations, keep the faith and keep reading God's word. Don't give up on all the things you are seeking from God. Don't give up on how you want to see yourself becoming now and in the future because God's timing is perfect and it's just for you.

The following are some key factors that will encourage and help you to become an even greater you:

- ❑ Pray daily.
- ❑ Speak affirmations.
- ❑ Start acting out in faith what you are speaking.
- ❑ Repent daily.
- ❑ Read the bible.

- ❏ Fast for spiritual strength.
- ❏ Meditate silently or with soft inspirational music.
- ❏ Attend physical or virtual bible study for spiritual strength.
- ❏ Surround yourself with Christian believers.
- ❏ Make lifestyle changes that are more positive and acceptable to God.
- ❏ Don't give up even if you get weak in trying.

Don't be afraid to reset your mind the way you've been thinking or the way you been speaking as it relates to yourself, circumstances or future.
If you desire to make a change you have to do it for yourself and with Gods help you can accomplish whatever it is you desire.

I am so excited for you because I know firsthand the key factors I have given you work. Also, the book is a tool to help jumpstart you on your path to overflowing blessings, your desired future and to becoming a better you and nothing or nobody can stop it.

Jumpstart and pass it on!